# Explode The Cc

*Essential lessons for phonics mastery*

Nancy Hall • Rena Price

EDUCATORS PUBLISHING SERVICE
Cambridge and Toronto

**Cover art:** Hugh Price
**Text illustrations:** Laura Price, Alan Price, Ann Iosa



Printed in Mayfield, PA, in October 2020
ISBN 978-0-8388-7803-3

7 8 9 10 PAH 24 23 22 21 20

Lesson 1

*a, e, i, o, u,* and sometimes *y* are vowels.

◯ the vowels.

| | |
|---|---|
| bat | it |
| rib | fed |
| club | bank |
| on | fat |
| tub | skunk |
| slap | box |

*a, e, i, o, u,* and sometimes *y* are vowels.
Sometimes vowels say their names.

◯ the vowel that says its name.

| | |
|---|---|
| 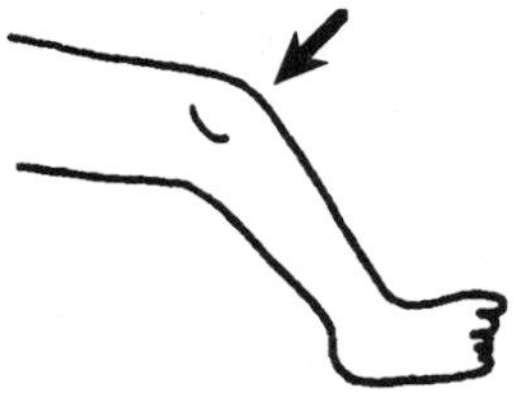 (e) i o |  i e o |
|  a o u |  i u a |
|  a i o |  u o e |
|  o a e |  e u o |

In each word below, the vowel says its name.

◯ the vowels.

| go | I |
|---|---|
| we | he |
| hi | so |
| no | be |

If a vowel is at the end of a little word,
the vowel says its name.

◯ it.

| | |
|---|---|
| me or men? | he or hen? |
| we or wet? | yes or yo-yo? |
| hill or hi? | no or net? |
| go or got? | bop or Bo? |

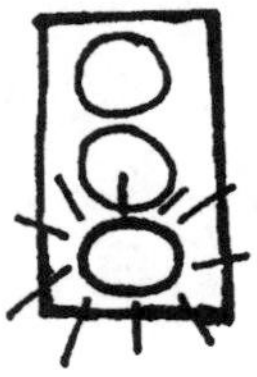

Read, write, and ◯ it.

| | | | |
|---|---|---|---|
| he<br>h e |  |  |  |
| we<br>__ __ |  |  | 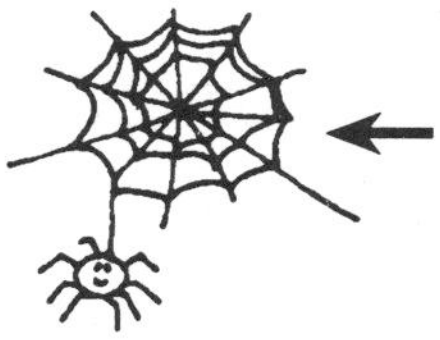 |
| go<br>__ __ |  |  | 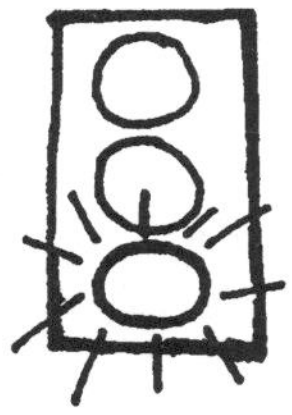 |
| me<br>__ __ |  |  |  |
| yo-yo<br>__ __-__ __ |  |  |  |
| hi<br>__ __ |  |  |  |
| no<br>__ __ |  |  |  |

If a little word ends in *y*, the *y* says /ī/.

◯ it.

| | |
|---|---|
|  drop or dry? |  trap or try? |
|  crib or cry? |  mitt or my? |
|  flat or fly? |  sky or skin? |
|  spy or spin? |  Fred or fry? |

Read, write, and ⬭ it.

| | | | |
|---|---|---|---|
| my<br>__ __ | | | |
| cry<br>__ __ __ | | | |
| fry<br>__ __ __ | | | |
| sky<br>__ __ __ | | | |
| spy<br>__ __ __ | | | |
| dry<br>__ __ __ | | | |
| fly<br>__ __ __ | | | |

Match and write it.

| sky | fry | ~~we~~ | yo-yo | no |
|---|---|---|---|---|
| me | go | cry | spy | fly |

we

Yes or no?

| | Yes | No |
|---|---|---|
| Can a sled fly in the sky? | ☐ | ☒ |
| Can he fry an egg in a pan? | ☐ | ☐ |
| Will Sam cry if he is sad? | ☐ | ☐ |
| Will we trap a bad spy? | ☐ | ☐ |
| Can a cat swim in the sky? | ☐ | ☐ |
| Will a rug try to go to bed? | ☐ | ☐ |
| Is a wet duck dry? | ☐ | ☐ |

Write it.

| | |
|---|---|
| 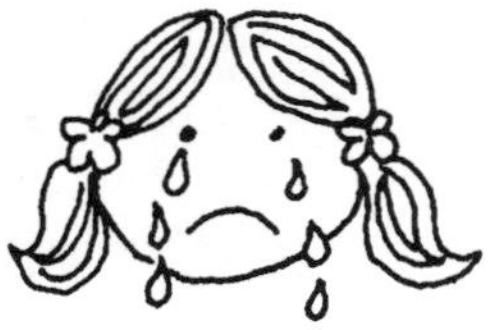 | cry |
| 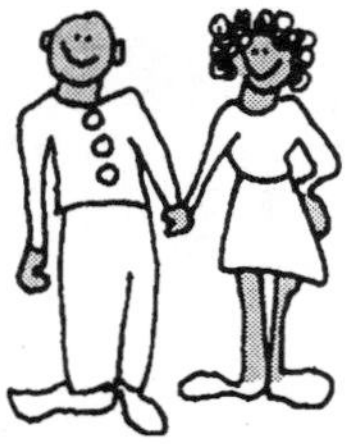 | |
| 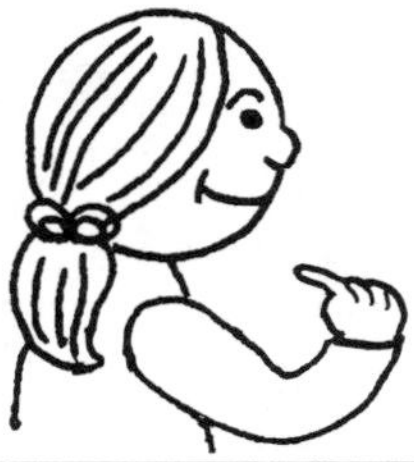 | |
| 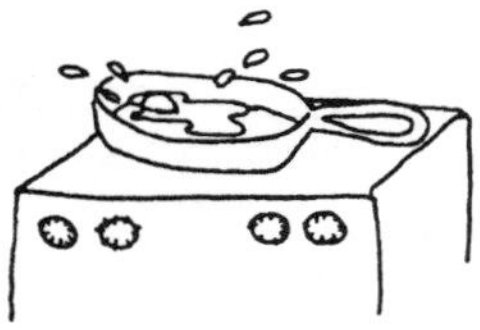 | |
|  | |
| 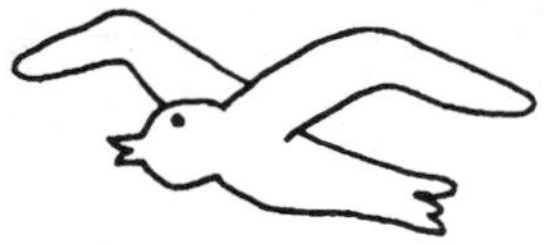 | |
| 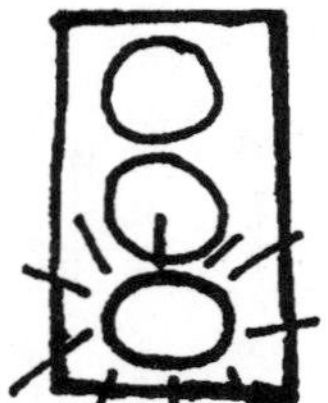 | |

Lesson 2

Put a silent *e* at the end of a word, and the vowel before it says its name.

Add a silent *e* to the words below.
Does your word fit the picture?

c u t → c u t e

m a d → ___ ___ ___ ___

c u b → ___ ___ ___ ___

T i m → ___ ___ ___ ___

c a p → ___ ___ ___ ___

If a word has silent *e* at the end, the vowel says its name.

◯ the vowel that says its name, and X the silent *e*.

| | |
|---|---|
| cute | made |
| home | here |
| line | cube |
| gate | pine |
| tube | pole |

Read, write, and ◯ it.

| | | | |
|---|---|---|---|
| cane<br>__ __ __ __ |  | |  |
| cute<br>__ __ __ __ |  |  |  |
| cape<br>__ __ __ __ |  |  |  |
| cube<br>__ __ __ __ | 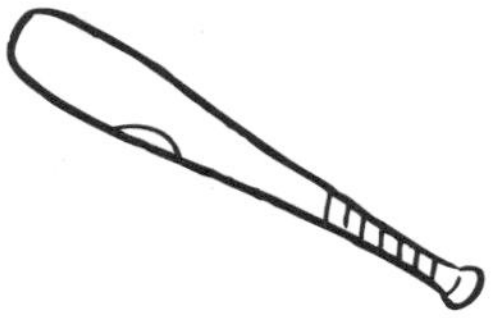 |  | 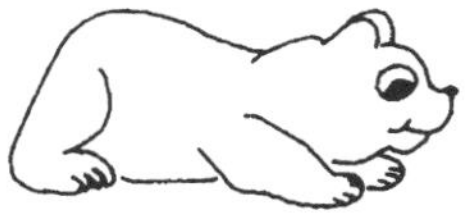 |
| pine<br>__ __ __ __ |  | 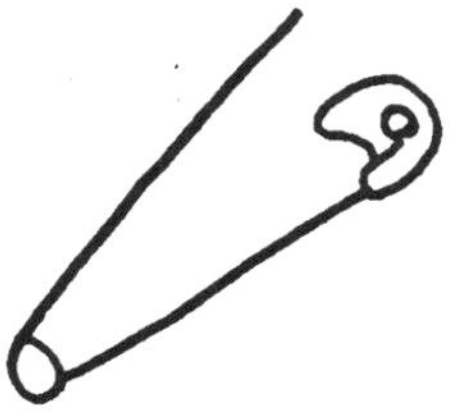 | 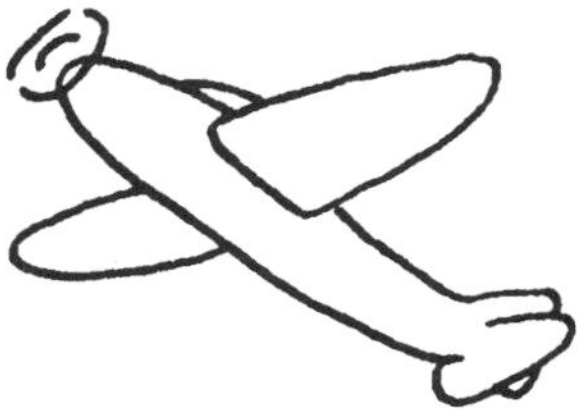 |
| made<br>__ __ __ __ |  |  |  |
| time<br>__ __ __ __ |  |  | 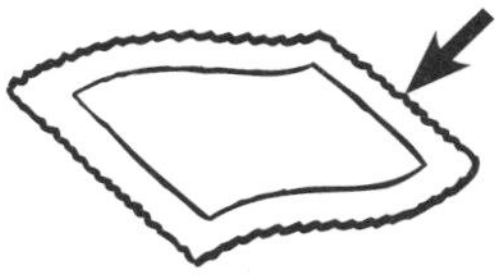 |

◯ it.

| | |
|---|---|
|  cap or cape? | 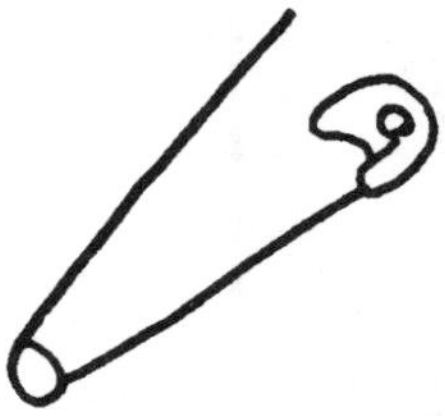 pin or pine? |
|  mad or made? |  cub or cube? |
| can or cane? |  cut or cute? |
|  cut or cute? |  cub or cube? |
|  cap or cape? |  mad or made? |

Match and write it.

| cane | cape | cub | cap | can |
|---|---|---|---|---|
| made | kite | time | cube | cute |

| | Spell. | | | Write. |
|---|---|---|---|---|
|  | (k) t | (i) e | (te) t | kite |
|  | s c | i a | p pe | |
|  | b c | u o | te t | |
|  | n m | i a | d de | |
| | g c | a o | n ne | |
|  | t p | u i | ne n | |
| 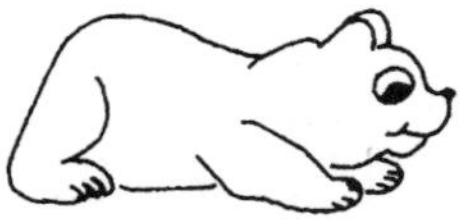 | b c | u o | be b | |

Yes or no?

| | Yes | No |
|---|---|---|
| Will a cape cry? | ☐ | ☐ |
| Can you put a cub in a glass? | ☐ | ☐ |
| Will a cat make its bed? | ☐ | ☐ |
| Do you fly a kite? | ☐ | ☐ |
| Will a crab use a cane? | ☐ | ☐ |
| Is a pine made of brass? | ☐ | ☐ |
| Is it time to go to bed? | ☐ | ☐ |

X it.

| | | |
|---|---|---|
| Sam has a cane and a cape. | ☐ |  |
| Sam has a cap in a can. | ☐ | |
| Pat made a red kite. | ☐ |  |
| Pat is mad at the cute cat. | ☐ | |
| Jim has the same pet as Jan. | ☐ |  |
| Jim has the same pot as Jan. | ☐ | |
| Ann has a cube in the glass. | ☐ |  |
| Ann has a cub in the glass. | ☐ | |
| Tim will fly in the sky. | ☐ |  |
| Time can go by fast. | ☐ | |
| The cute duck will try to swim. | ☐ |  |
| The duck will try to cut the bun. | ☐ | |
| The big clock has no hands. | ☐ |  |
| Tim tells the clock his plan. | ☐ | |

Write it.

Lesson 3

| | |
|---|---|
| ◯ it. tub<br>tube<br>tab | Sam<br>same<br>sand |
| robe<br>Rob<br>rode | tub<br>tap<br>tube |
| rob<br>robe<br>rode | ham<br>hog<br>home |
| rat<br>rake<br>rate | rod<br>rope<br>rode |
| hill<br>pole<br>pile | cone<br>cat<br>cake |

 it.

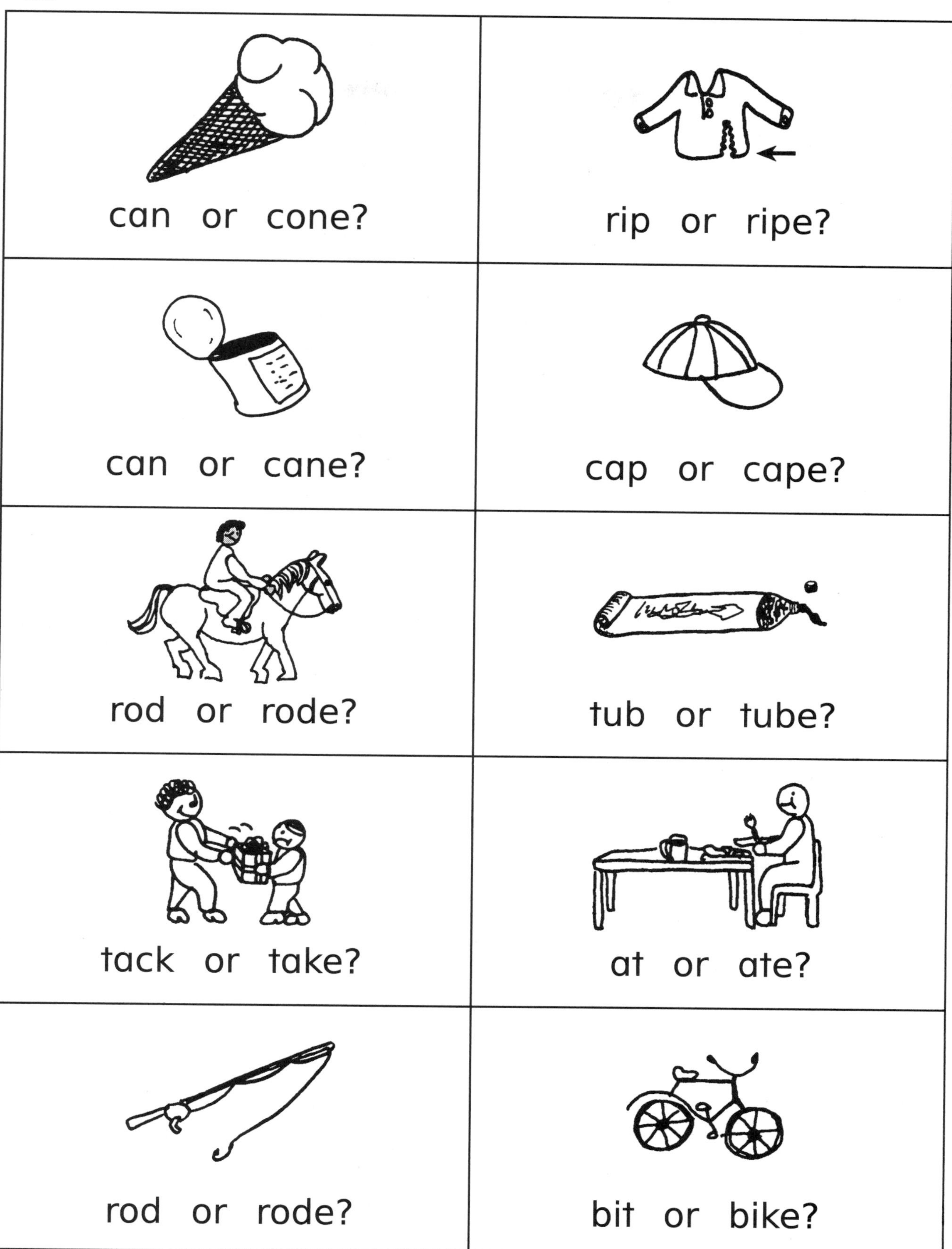
can or cone?
rip or ripe?
can or cane?
cap or cape?
rod or rode?
tub or tube?
tack or take?
at or ate?
rod or rode?
bit or bike?

Read, write, and ◯ it.

| | | | |
|---|---|---|---|
| bike<br>_ _ _ _ |  |  |  |
| tube<br>_ _ _ _ |  |  |  |
| rod<br>_ _ _ | 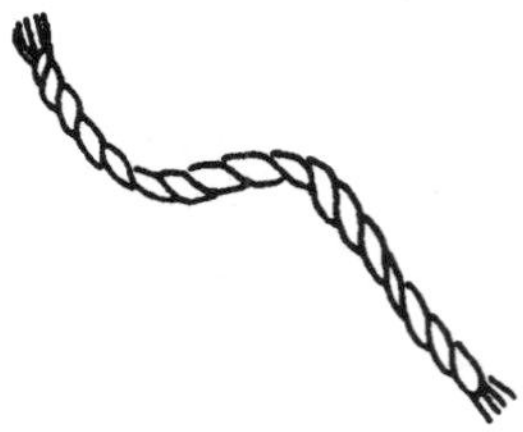 |  |  |
| cake<br>_ _ _ _ |  |  |  |
| game<br>_ _ _ _ |  |  | 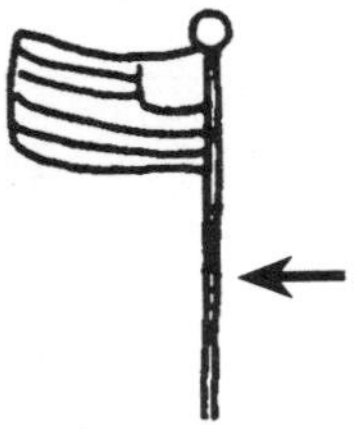 |
| lake<br>_ _ _ _ |  |  |  |
| home<br>_ _ _ _ |  |  |  |

Match and write it.

| home | lake | tube | rope | cone |
|---|---|---|---|---|
| cake | take | rake | ate | same |

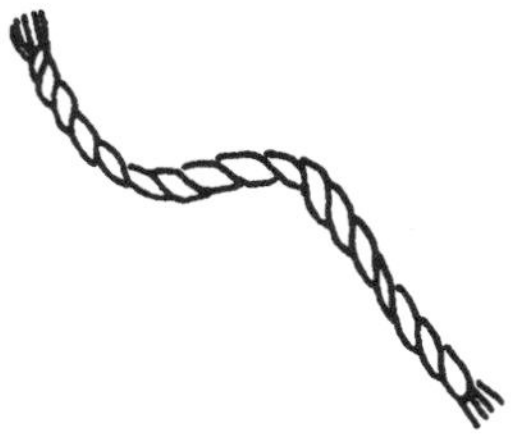

| | Spell. | | | | | | Write. |
|---|---|---|---|---|---|---|---|
| | t | c | a | u | ck | ke | |
| | t | c | u | o | be | b | |
| | b | p | i | a | ke | te | |
| | c | r | a | u | ck | ke | |
| | t | p | u | i | be | b | |
| | n | r | a | o | d | pe | |
| | c | s | o | i | me | ne | |

Yes or no?

| | Yes | No |
|---|---|---|
| Can you swim in a lake? | ☐ | ☐ |
| Can a plum be ripe? | ☐ | ☐ |
| Will a cake fly in the sky? | ☐ | ☐ |
| Is it fun to ride a bike? | ☐ | ☐ |
| Will a doll lick a cone? | ☐ | ☐ |
| Can a kite fit in a pipe? | ☐ | ☐ |
| Can you rope a fly? | ☐ | ☐ |

X it.

| | | |
|---|---|---|
| We will swim in the lake.<br><br>We will sled on the lake. | ☐<br><br>☐ | |
| Sal rode in a pine tub.<br><br>Sal rode on a fat tube. | ☐<br><br>☐ | |
| The twins ate the same cake.<br><br>The twins ate the same cape. | ☐<br><br>☐ | |
| Brad grabs the cone.<br><br>The frog licks the cone. | ☐<br><br>☐ | |
| Tom will rake a big pile.<br><br>Tom is still ill. | ☐<br><br>☐ | |
| Jane gave a cake to Dad.<br><br>Dad gave a pet to Jane. | ☐<br><br>☐ | |
| Fred rode home in his truck.<br><br>A fox rode home on Fred's bike. | ☐<br><br>☐ | |

Write it.

| | |
|---|---|
| ⬭ it. flame flap flip | mile smile stile |
| stop stove stone | slide smell snarl |
| plant plate plane | smoke smock snore |
| drip drive dive | stone stack stove |
| flap flake lake | broke bride blade |

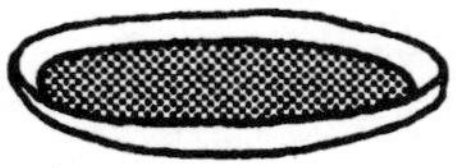

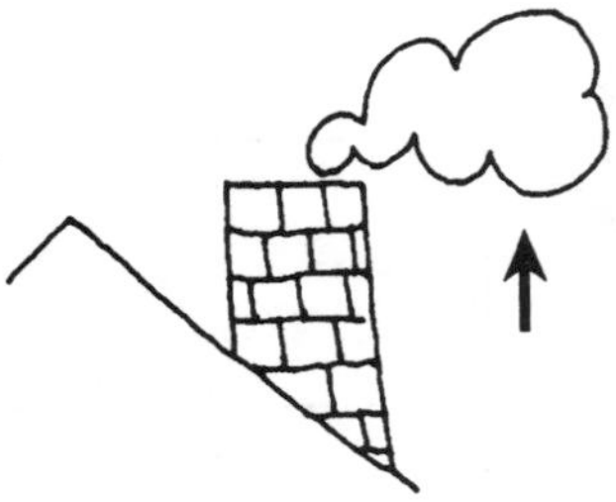

◯ it.

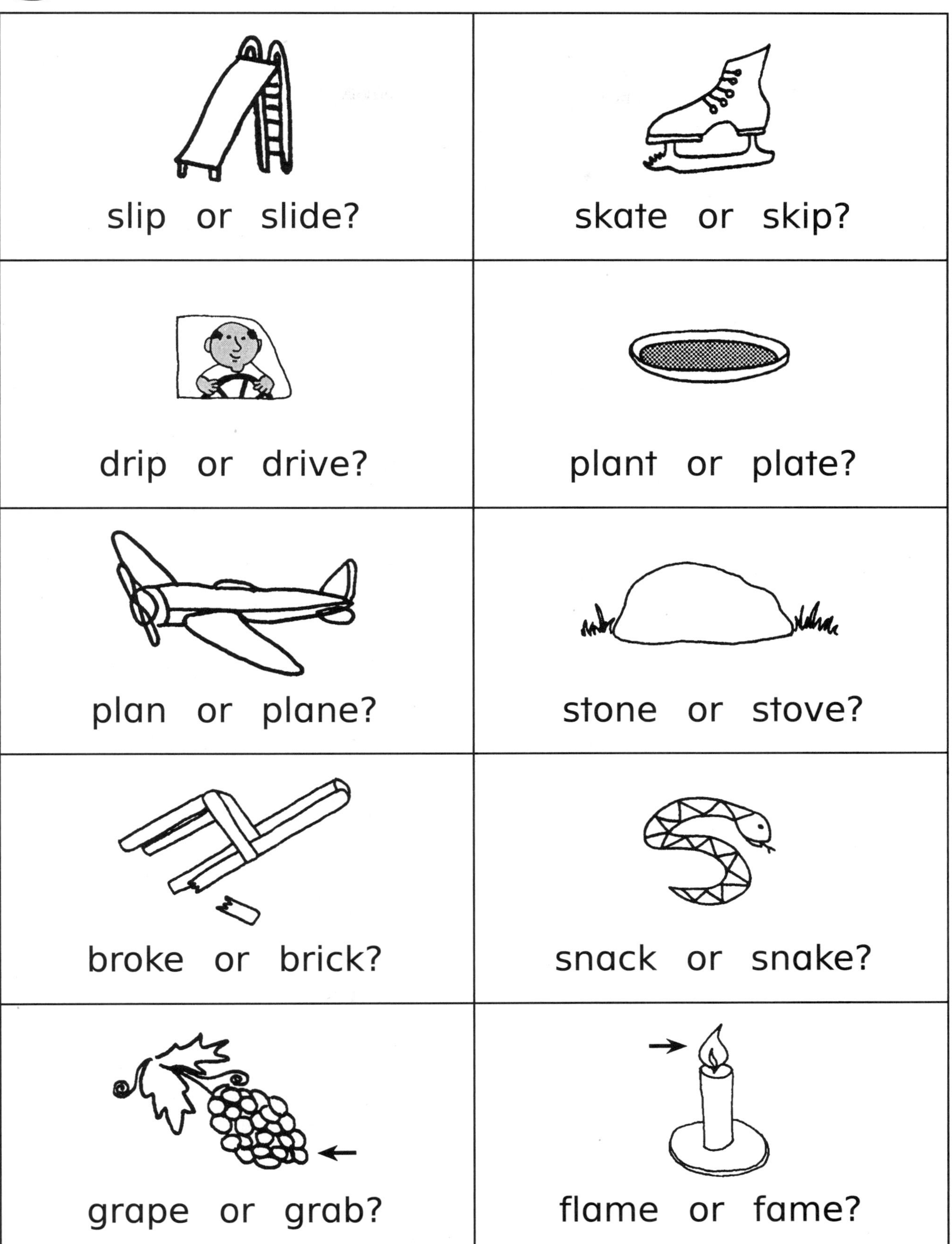
slip or slide?
skate or skip?
drip or drive?
plant or plate?
plan or plane?
stone or stove?
broke or brick?
snack or snake?
grape or grab?
flame or fame?

Read, write, and ⬭ it.

| | | | |
|---|---|---|---|
| plate<br>_ _ _ _ _ |  | 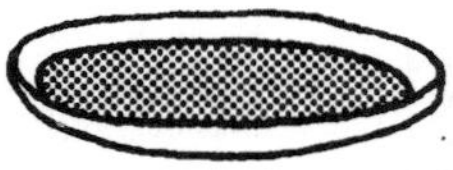 |  |
| stone<br>_ _ _ _ _ | 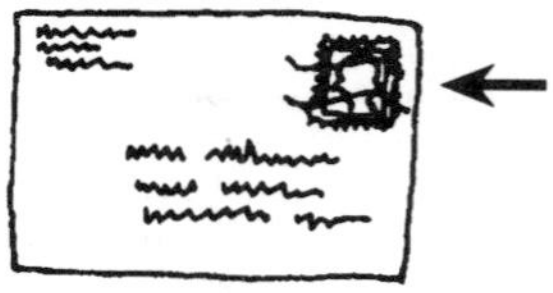 |  |  |
| stove<br>_ _ _ _ _ |  |  | 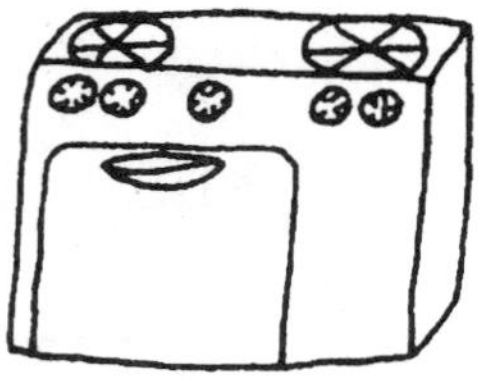 |
| smoke<br>_ _ _ _ _ |  |  |  |
| plane<br>_ _ _ _ _ | 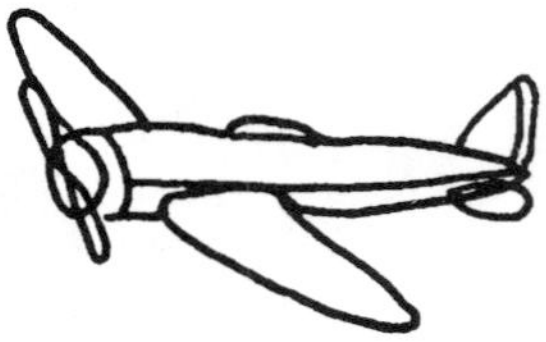 |  | 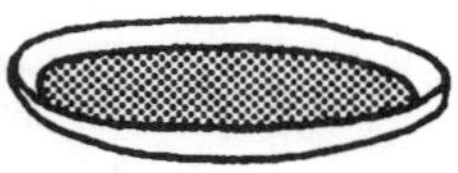 |
| broke<br>_ _ _ _ _ |  |  | 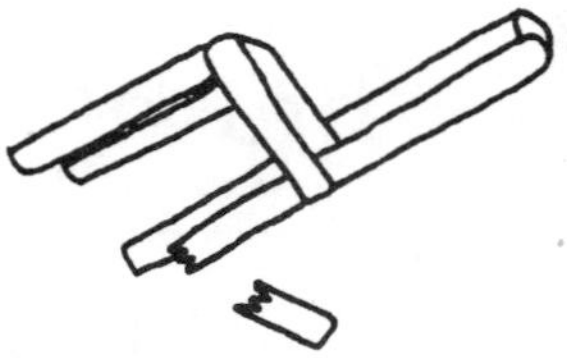 |
| skate<br>_ _ _ _ _ |  |  |  |

Match and write it.

| smile | drive | snake | grape | plane |
|---|---|---|---|---|
| slide | stove | skate | broke | stone |

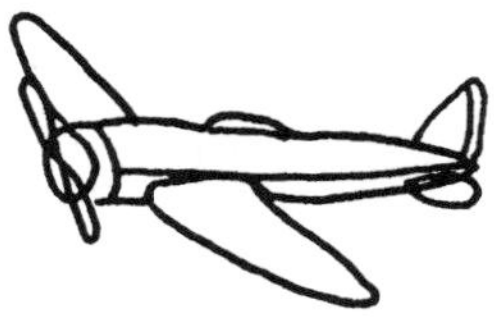

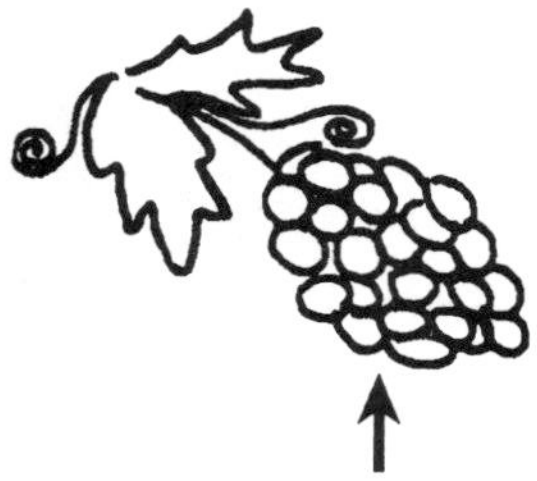

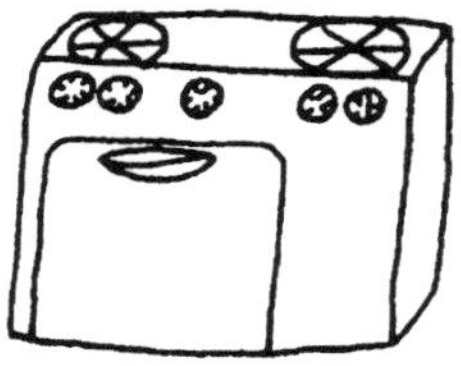

| | Spell. | | | Write. |
|---|---|---|---|---|
|  | sm  st | o  a | ne  n | |
|  | sl  st | o  i | ck  de | |
|  | sp  sn | o  a | ke  ne | |
|  | sm  sk | a  o | te  ke | |
|  | st  sn | i  a | ck  ke | |
|  | sm  sl | a  i | le  me | |
| 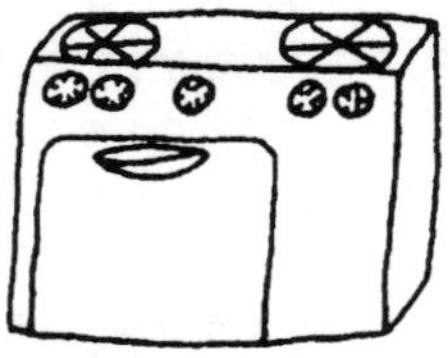 | st  sm | o  e | v  ve | |

Yes or no?

| | Yes | No |
|---|---|---|
| Can you slip on a slide? | ☐ | ☐ |
| Will Tom smile if he is sad? | ☐ | ☐ |
| Can Jane drive home? | ☐ | ☐ |
| Can you skate on a plate? | ☐ | ☐ |
| Will you get a snake as a snack? | ☐ | ☐ |
| Can you make smoke with a fire? | ☐ | ☐ |
| Can a cat slide into home plate? | ☐ | ☐ |

X it.

| | |
|---|---|
| Steve will not smile. ☐<br><br>Steve will not smell. ☐ |  |
| Kate can fly a plane. ☐<br><br>Kate drove up the steps. ☐ |  |
| Fred skates in the game. ☐<br><br>Fred skips by the gate. ☐ |  |
| The plate broke on the stove. ☐<br><br>The pipe broke the stone. ☐ | 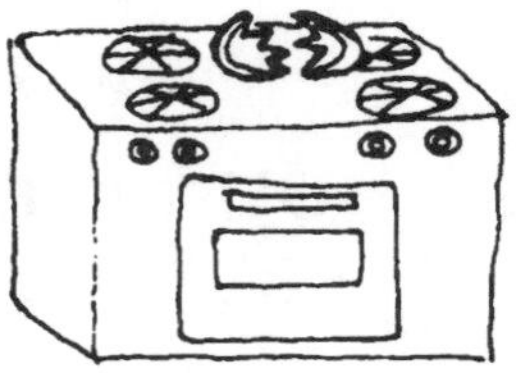 |
| The plate will fly in the sky. ☐<br><br>The cute fly has a plane. ☐ |  |
| The snake smiles at Dave. ☐<br><br>Dave smells the snack. ☐ |  |
| The snake slid on the steps. ☐<br><br>The slide has a sock on it. ☐ |  |

Write it.

*sh* says /sh/ as in *sh*<u></u>*ell.*

the picture that begins with /sh/.

| | | | |
|---|---|---|---|
| sh- | | | |
| sh- | | | |
| sh- | | | |

Listen for /sh/ at the end as in *fish*.

the picture that ends with /sh/.

| | | | |
|---|---|---|---|
| -sh | | | |
| -sh | | | |
| -sh | | | |

 it.

| | |
|---|---|
| shot<br>shop<br>ship | ship<br>shell<br>sell |
| dash<br>brush<br>dish | crust<br>crash<br>crush |
| hut<br>shut<br>shop | share<br>save<br>shave |
| cash<br>crash<br>crust | shed<br>shot<br>sled |
| rust<br>rash<br>rush | track<br>trash<br>truck |

Read, write, and ◯ it.

| | | | |
|---|---|---|---|
| shade<br>_ _ _ _ _ |  |  |  |
| shop<br>_ _ _ _ |  |  |  |
| shell<br>_ _ _ _ _ |  |  |  |
| ship<br>_ _ _ _ |  |  |  |
| fish<br>_ _ _ _ |  |  | 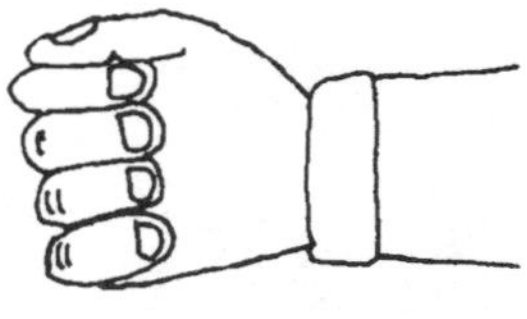 |
| dish<br>_ _ _ _ |  |  | 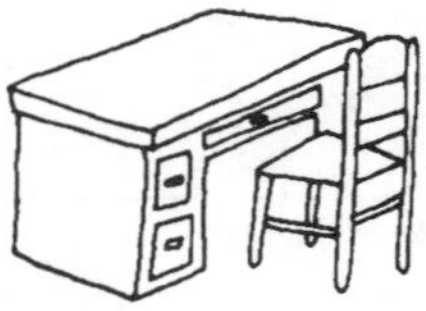 |
| shine<br>_ _ _ _ _ |  |  | 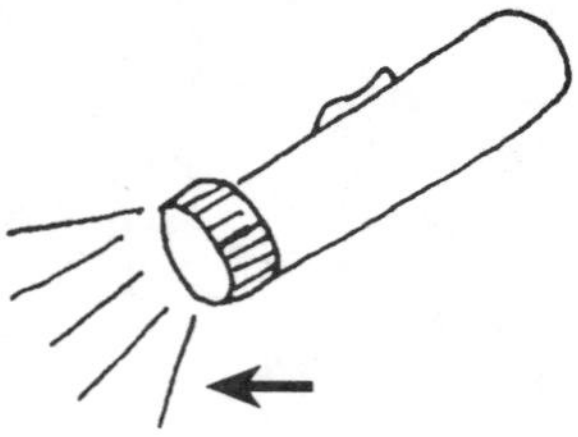 |

Match and write it.

| dish | ship | brush | shed | shave |
|---|---|---|---|---|
| crash | shell | shop | shade | shine |

| | Spell. | | | Write. |
|---|---|---|---|---|
|  | st sh | e a | lt ll | |
|  | f g | a i | m sh | |
|  | st sh | a o | p d | |
|  | sn sh | e u | d t | |
|  | sh sl | a o | pe ve | |
| 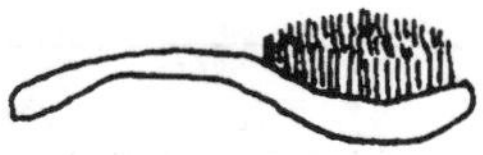 | gr br | o u | st sh | |
|  | cr c | i a | sh ss | |

Yes or no?

| | Yes | No |
|---|---|---|
| Is a ship big? | ☐ | ☐ |
| Will a shell trot? | ☐ | ☐ |
| Can a dish shave? | ☐ | ☐ |
| Can I brush a pet? | ☐ | ☐ |
| Can a ship grin? | ☐ | ☐ |
| Will a fish swim well? | ☐ | ☐ |
| Can a sled crash on a hill? | ☐ | ☐ |

X it.

| | |
|---|---|
| The shell is big. ☐<br>The shed is big. ☐ | 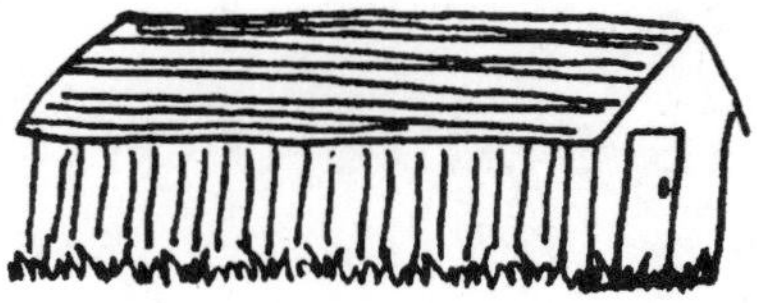 |
| A cute fish is in the dish. ☐<br>A cute fish is on the ship. ☐ |  |
| The lake will shine in the sun. ☐<br>Jane will stand in the shade. ☐ |  |
| Jeff will try to brush the fish. ☐<br>Jeff will dry the brush in the sun. ☐ | 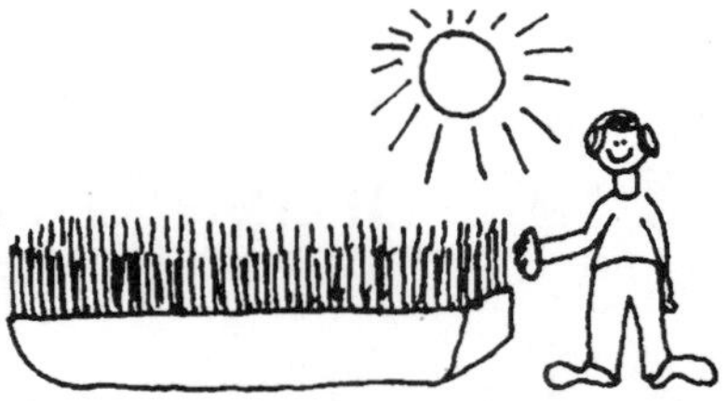 |
| The flat plate can crack if it drops. ☐<br>The fat plane will crash if it flips. ☐ |  |
| My brush has a smile. ☐<br>My brush has a smell. ☐ | 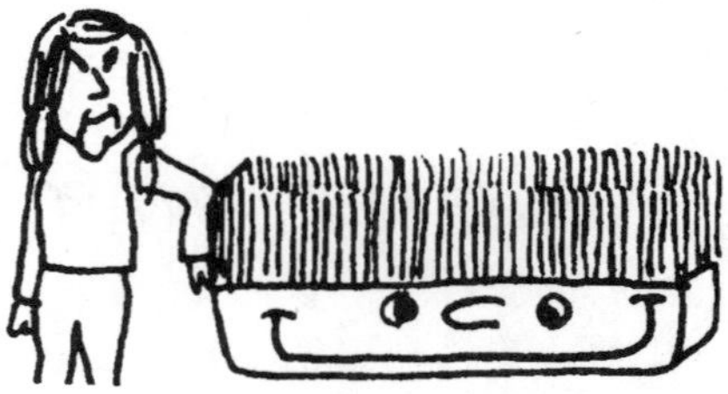 |
| Dave drove his bike in the sand. ☐<br>Dave rode his bike in the trash. ☐ |  |

Write it.

Lesson 6

*th* says /th/ as in *thumb*.

◯ the picture that begins with /th/.

| | | | |
|---|---|---|---|
| th- |  |  |  |
| th- | 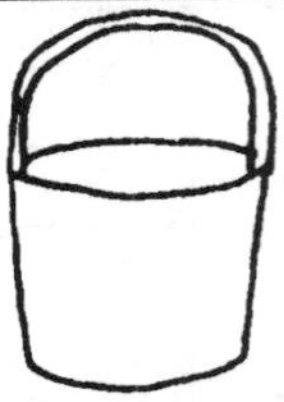 |  |  |
| th- |  |  |  |

*wh* says /wh/ as in *wheel*.

◯ the picture that begins with /wh/.

| | | | |
|---|---|---|---|
| wh- | 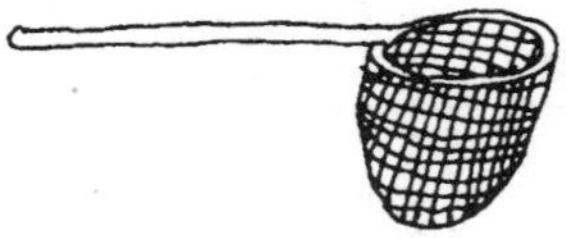 |  |  |
| wh- |  |  | 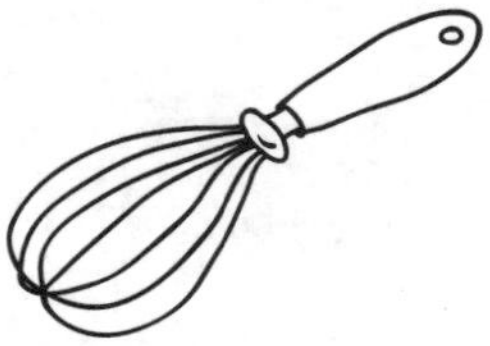 |
| wh- |  |  |  |

◯ it.

| | |
|---|---|
| 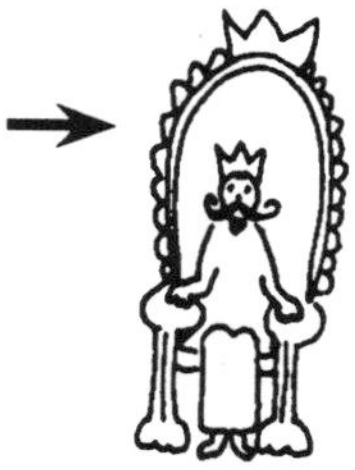 throne<br>tone<br>trot |  bat<br>bath<br>path |
|  bath<br>path<br>pats |  bath<br>brat<br>bat |
|  think<br>trick<br>tick | 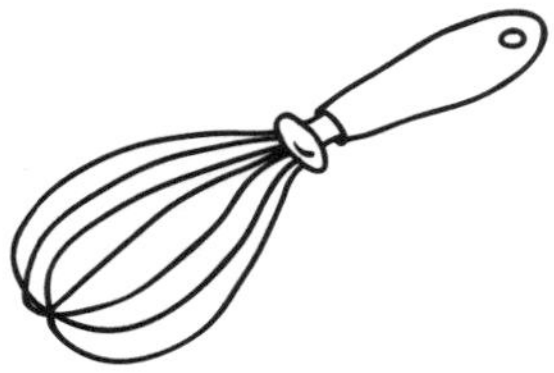 whisk<br>which<br>wins |
| 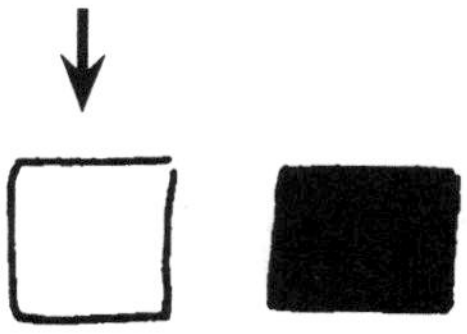 white<br>wit<br>while |  whale<br>wham<br>when |
| 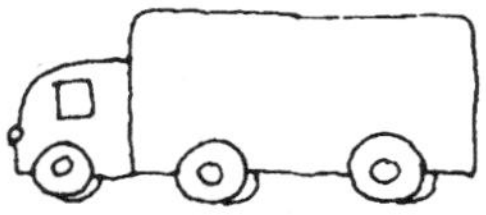 truck<br>trash<br>trip |  thin<br>think<br>thick |

Read, write, and it.

| | | | |
|---|---|---|---|
| them<br>_ _ _ _ |  |  |  |
| think<br>_ _ _ _ _ |  |  |  |
| thin<br>_ _ _ _ |  | 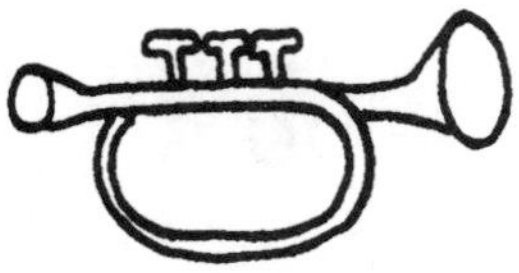 |  |
| math<br>_ _ _ _ |  | 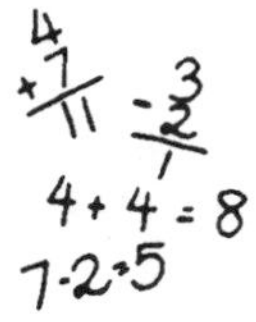 |  |
| wham<br>_ _ _ _ |  |  | 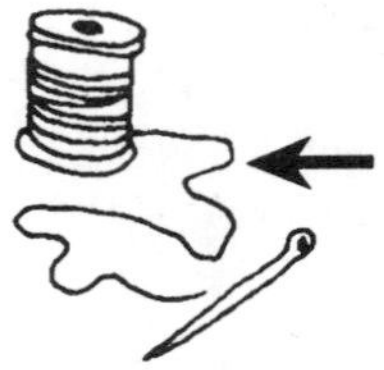 |
| whine<br>_ _ _ _ _ |  |  |  |
| white<br>_ _ _ _ _ |  |  | 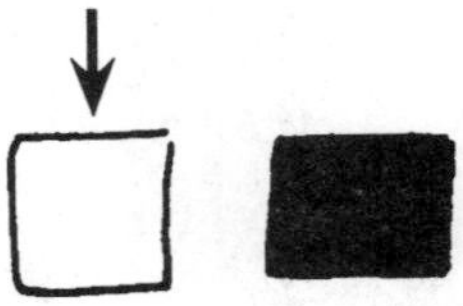 |

Match and write it.

| | | | | |
|---|---|---|---|---|
| whisk | think | when | bath | thin |
| thick | white | math | whale | path |

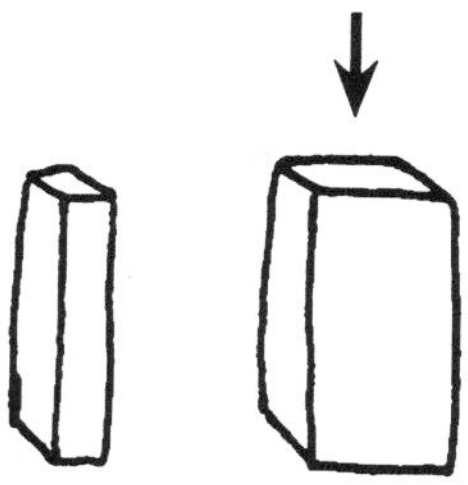

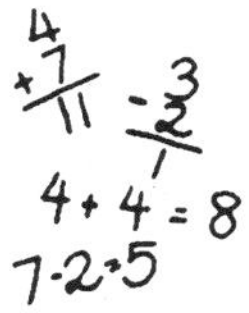

4
+7
11

3
-2
1

4 + 4 = 8
7-2=5

| | Spell. | | | Write. |
|---|---|---|---|---|
|  | th sh | e i | nk s | |
|  | th wh | a i | sk m | |
|  | p m | i a | ll th | |
|  | d b | o a | th lt | |
| 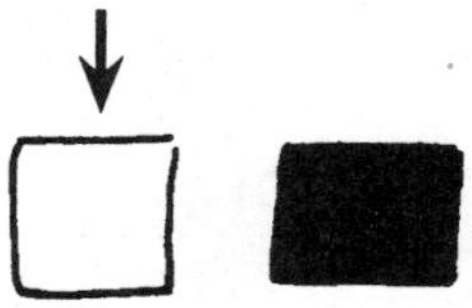 | v wh | i e | le te | |
|  | wh sh | o a | le p | |
|  | wh th | i a | nk n | |

Yes or no?

| | Yes | No |
|---|---|---|
| Can a whale swim? | ☐ | ☐ |
| Will a throne shave? | ☐ | ☐ |
| Can a whisk think? | ☐ | ☐ |
| Can a dress be white? | ☐ | ☐ |
| Will a clock take a bath? | ☐ | ☐ |
| Can a path go to my home? | ☐ | ☐ |
| Will a fish grab a whale? | ☐ | ☐ |

X it.

| | | |
|---|---|---|
| The pet did math.<br>The pet had a bath. | ☐<br>☐ | |
| Tim gave me thin socks.<br>Tim gave me a white box. | ☐<br>☐ | |
| A rake is on the path.<br>A cake is in the bath. | ☐<br>☐ | |
| The snack is in the whale.<br>The whale is in the shed. | ☐<br>☐ | |
| Mat is on the slide.<br>Math is in the sky. | ☐<br>☐ | |
| Sam whisks the cake to mix it.<br>Sam whips a stick in the lake. | ☐<br>☐ | |
| Pat and Pam share the stove.<br>Pam pats the snake. | ☐<br>☐ | |

Write it.

## Lesson 7

*ch* says /ch/ as in *<u>ch</u>air*.

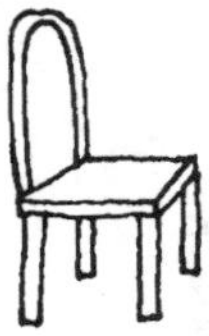

◯ the picture that begins with /ch/.

| | | | |
|---|---|---|---|
| ch- | 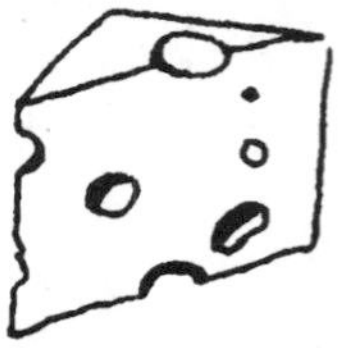 | 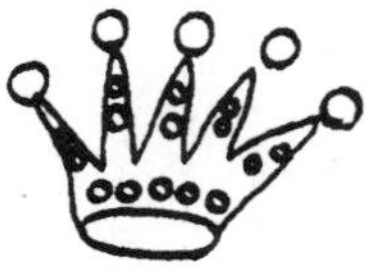 | 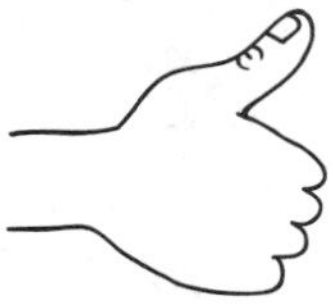 |
| ch- | 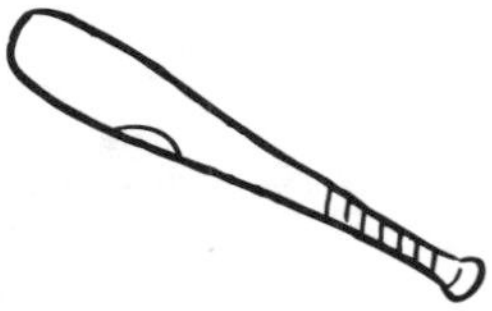 | 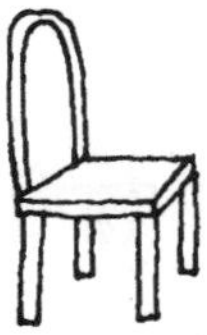 | 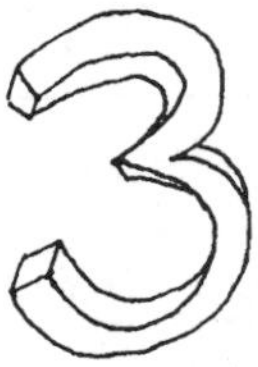 |
| ch- | 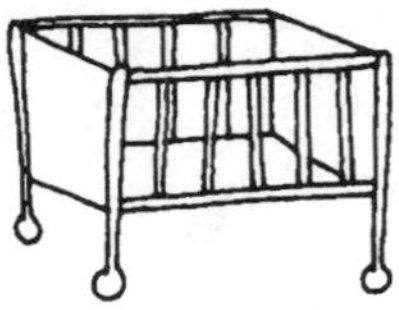 | 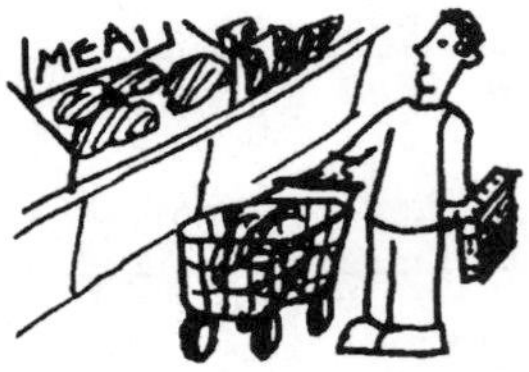  | 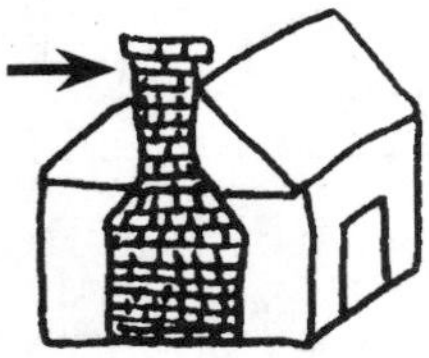 |

*-tch* at the end of a word says /ch/ as in *wa<u>tch</u>*.

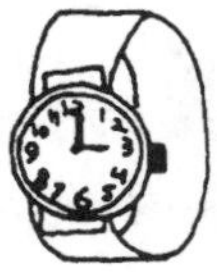

◯ the picture that ends with /ch/.

| | | | |
|---|---|---|---|
| -tch | 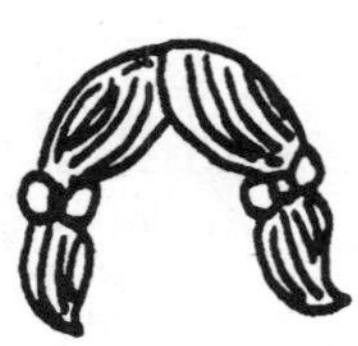 | 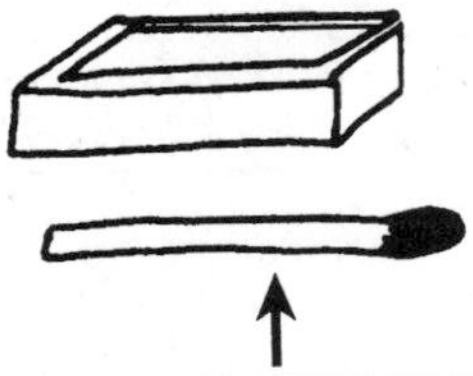 | 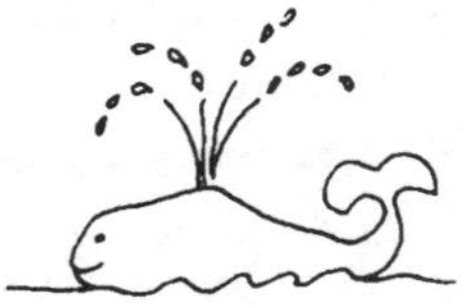 |
| -tch | 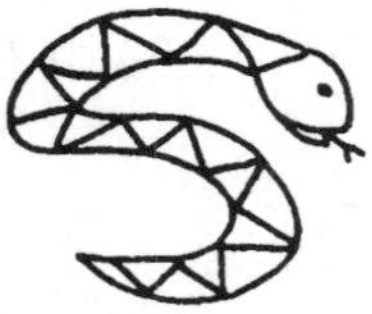 | 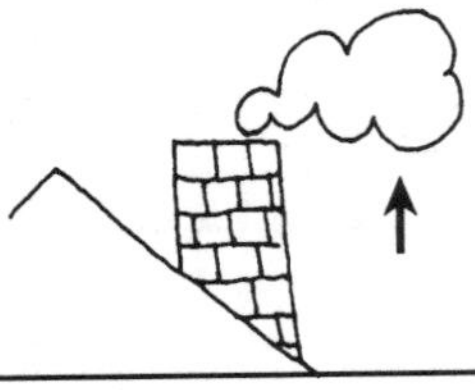 | 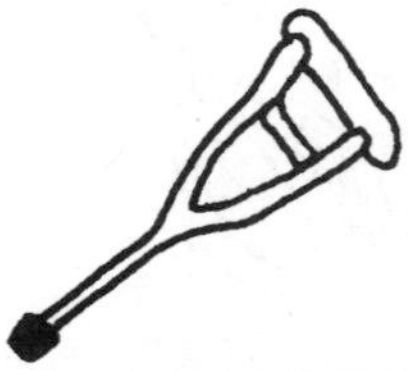 |
| -tch | 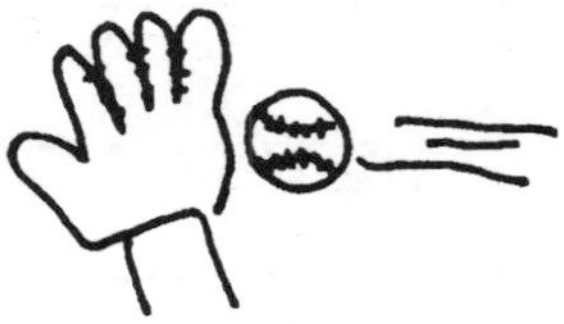 | 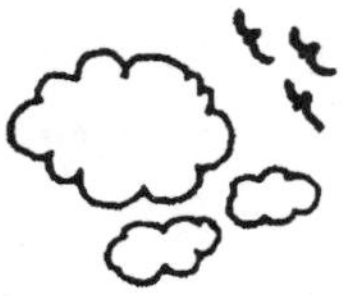 | 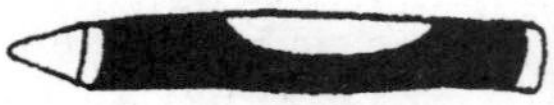 |

 it.

| | |
|---|---|
| chick<br>chuck<br>catch | chop<br>class<br>chess |
| clap<br>chip<br>ship | pitch<br>patch<br>punch |
| chin<br>chill<br>shell | lunch<br>bunch<br>land |
| bent<br>bank<br>bench | watch<br>whisk<br>wick |
| crash<br>chair<br>chess | catch<br>chick<br>crutch |

Read, write, and (circle) it.

| | | | |
|---|---|---|---|
| punch<br>_ _ _ _ _ | | | |
| chin<br>_ _ _ _ | | | |
| chop<br>_ _ _ _ | | | |
| inch<br>_ _ _ _ | 1 2 3 | | |
| chess<br>_ _ _ _ _ | | | |
| rich<br>_ _ _ _ | | | |
| crutch<br>_ _ _ _ _ _ | | | |

Match and write it.

| chess | chop | catch | bench | patch |
| --- | --- | --- | --- | --- |
| chip | chin | chick | lunch | chill |

| | Spell. | | | | | | Write. |
|---|---|---|---|---|---|---|---|
|  | th | ch | e | i | ss | ll | |
| 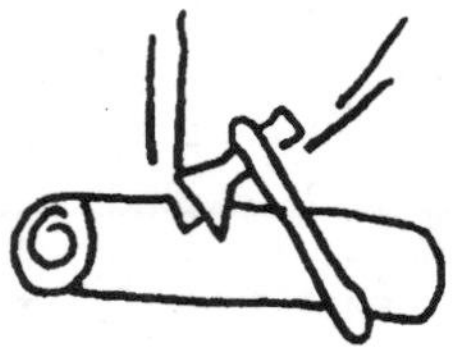 | ch | cl | o | e | t | p | |
|  | th | ch | u | i | ll | f | |
|  | c | s | a | o | th | tch | |
|  | p | r | i | a | sh | ch | |
| 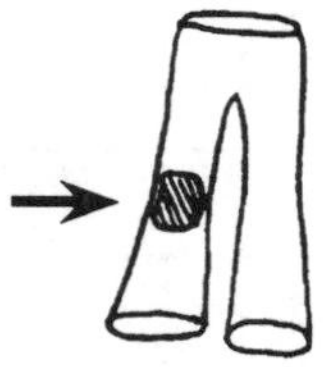 | d | p | a | o | tch | ck | |
| 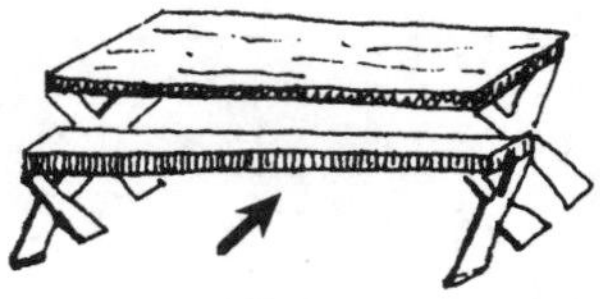 | m | b | a | en | ct | ch | |

Yes or no?

| | Yes | No |
|---|---|---|
| Can a dish chop a stone? | ☐ | ☐ |
| Will a bench skip? | ☐ | ☐ |
| Can a patch be on a dress? | ☐ | ☐ |
| Can a chick catch a bug? | ☐ | ☐ |
| Can you drink punch in a hut? | ☐ | ☐ |
| Can a pet use a crutch? | ☐ | ☐ |
| Will lunch be on a fish? | ☐ | ☐ |

X it.

| | | |
|---|---|---|
| Jen has a chill.<br><br>Jen has a chin. | ☐<br><br>☐ | |
| Chet will pick up the crutch.<br><br>I will hop on a crutch. | ☐<br><br>☐ | |
| Chaz will fly a kite at the lake.<br><br>The fish will try to catch the frog. | ☐<br><br>☐ | |
| Chet will crash on the bench.<br><br>Chet can catch the jet. | ☐<br><br>☐ | |
| Hope has a white plane.<br><br>Hope has a white plate. | ☐<br><br>☐ | |
| Mitch will try to patch the dish.<br><br>Mitch will try to punch the gate. | ☐<br><br>☐ | |
| Bet drinks pink punch.<br><br>Bet stands by the bench. | ☐<br><br>☐ | |

Write it.

## Lesson 8

*-ng* says /ng/ as in *ri<u>ng</u>*.

⬭ the picture that ends with /ng/.

| | | | |
|---|---|---|---|
| -ng | | | |
| -ng | | | |
| -ng | | | |

*-ck* says /k/ as in *clo<u>ck</u>*.

⬭ the picture that ends with /k/.

| | | | |
|---|---|---|---|
| -ck | | | |
| -ck | | | |
| -ck | | | |

◯ it.

| | |
|---|---|
| tack<br>track<br>tick | sing<br>ring<br>rind |
| gag<br>gang<br>rang | wing<br>rang<br>wind |
| think<br>bring<br>thing | lock<br>log<br>lack |
| mock<br>neck<br>nest | sick<br>stuck<br>stick |
| sting<br>king<br>sling | swim<br>sink<br>swing |

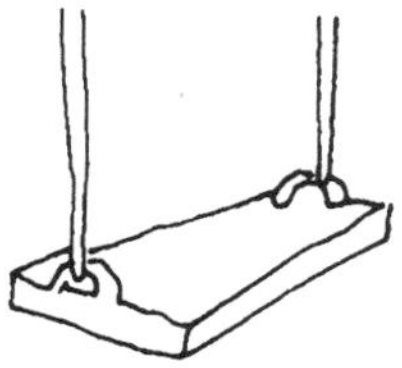

Read, write, and ⬭ it.

| | | | |
|---|---|---|---|
| king<br>___ ___ ___ ___ |  |  |  |
| ring<br>___ ___ ___ ___ |  |  |  |
| sing<br>___ ___ ___ ___ |  |  |  |
| chick<br>___ ___ ___ ___ ___ |  |  |  |
| tack<br>___ ___ ___ ___ |  |  |  |
| sick<br>___ ___ ___ ___ |  |  |  |
| hang<br>___ ___ ___ ___ | 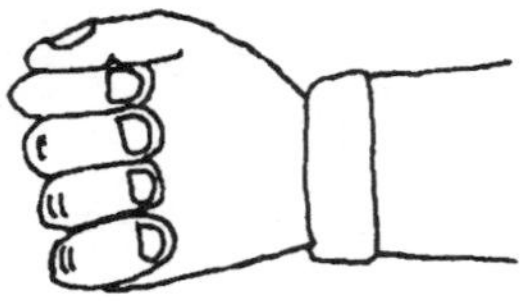 |  |  |

Match and write it.

| | | | | |
|---|---|---|---|---|
| hang | sting | chick | sing | tack |
| lock | ring | neck | wing | swing |

| | Spell. | | | Write. |
|---|---|---|---|---|
|  | t r | i o | ng nt | |
|  | st sh | u i | ng m | |
|  | b h | a o | n ng | |
| 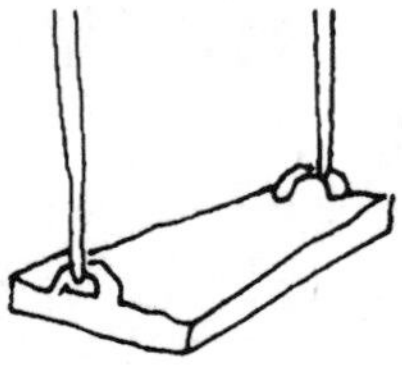 | sm sw | i e | nt ng | |
|  | ch th | a i | ss ck | |
|  | s st | i e | ck ng | |
|  | m n | e a | ss ck | |

Yes or no?

| | Yes | No |
| --- | --- | --- |
| Can a gang sing? | ☐ | ☐ |
| Will a ring like a snack? | ☐ | ☐ |
| Will a stick take a bath? | ☐ | ☐ |
| Will a chick have a wing? | ☐ | ☐ |
| Can a lock sing to me? | ☐ | ☐ |
| Can I hang a map up with a tack? | ☐ | ☐ |
| Will a swing fit in a sock? | ☐ | ☐ |

X it.

| | | |
|---|---|---|
| Ted has a sting.<br><br>Ted can sing. | ☐<br><br>☐ | |
| A wing is on the king.<br><br>A ring is on the clock. | ☐<br><br>☐ | |
| The trap hangs on the nest.<br><br>The tag hangs on my neck. | ☐<br><br>☐ | |
| The swing is on the shack.<br><br>The swing is on the snake. | ☐<br><br>☐ | |
| It takes a long time to fix the lock.<br><br>It will not take long to set the clock. | ☐<br><br>☐ | |
| A whale can swim well.<br><br>A class can sing on a rock. | ☐<br><br>☐ | |
| The fat frog has lunch.<br><br>The fast chick can punch. | ☐<br><br>☐ | |

Write it.

| | |
|---|---|
| it.<br>shack<br>snake<br>shake | pack<br>junk<br>joke |
| Mitch<br>mash<br>match | ding-dong<br>sing-song<br>ping-pong |
| sack<br>snack<br>snake | snare<br>shape<br>shore |
| which<br>whine<br>wind | scare<br>skip<br>store |
| chase<br>check<br>case | rose<br>frame<br>froze |

Read and ⬭ it.

| | | | |
|---|---|---|---|
|  | check | chess | such |
|  | snack | snatch | snake |
| 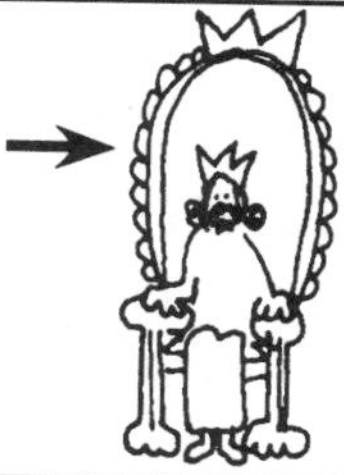 | throne | throb | shone |
|  | crash | track | trash |
|  | check | catch | chick |
|  | struck | strong | sting |
| 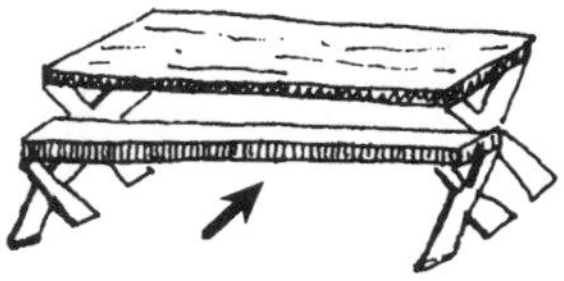 | branch | such | bench |

Read, write, and ◯ it.

| | | | |
|---|---|---|---|
| whine<br>_ _ _ _ _ | | | |
| shape<br>_ _ _ _ _ | | | |
| snake<br>_ _ _ _ _ | | | |
| tick-tock<br>_ _ _ _-_ _ _ _ | | | |
| shine<br>_ _ _ _ _ | | | |
| white<br>_ _ _ _ _ | | | |
| match<br>_ _ _ _ _ | | | |

| | Spell. | | | Write. |
|---|---|---|---|---|
|  | sh sn | a o | le ke | |
| 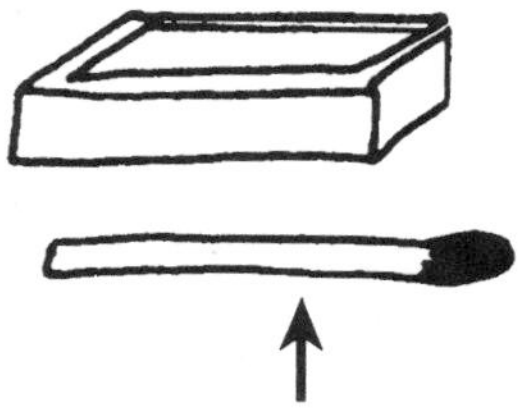 | w m | i a | tch sh | |
|  | ch sh | e a | ck ne | |
|  | tr thr | u o | ne ng | |
|  | sh ch | i e | ss st | |
| 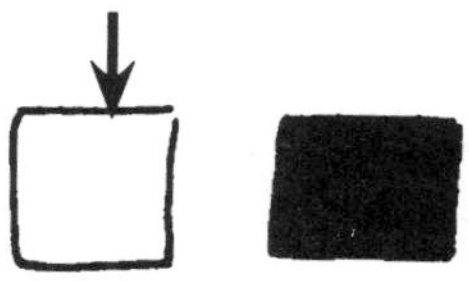 | wh th | a i | le te | |
|  | str sh | i o | mp ng | |

Yes or no?

| | Yes | No |
|---|---|---|
| Will a stick whine? | ☐ | ☐ |
| Can Mitch tell a joke? | ☐ | ☐ |
| Can we drive to the joke shop? | ☐ | ☐ |
| Is a match glad to shave? | ☐ | ☐ |
| Will a fish go tick-tock? | ☐ | ☐ |
| Can I shake a leg? | ☐ | ☐ |
| Will a bench chase a whale? | ☐ | ☐ |

X it.

| | | |
|---|---|---|
| A match can smile.<br>A mat can doze. | ☐<br>☐ | |
| The cake froze in the cube.<br>The cube froze on the skate. | ☐<br>☐ | |
| The pup will smile at lunch.<br>The pup swims to lunch. | ☐<br>☐ | |
| A snake sits on the stove.<br>The white clock is on sale. | ☐<br>☐ | SALE |
| Jane will try to catch the pet.<br>Jane made a sketch of Pete. | ☐<br>☐ | |
| The bike can chase the class.<br>The class will chase the kite. | ☐<br>☐ | |
| A fish can tell a cute joke.<br>Tish can sell a fine rake. | ☐<br>☐ | |

Write it.

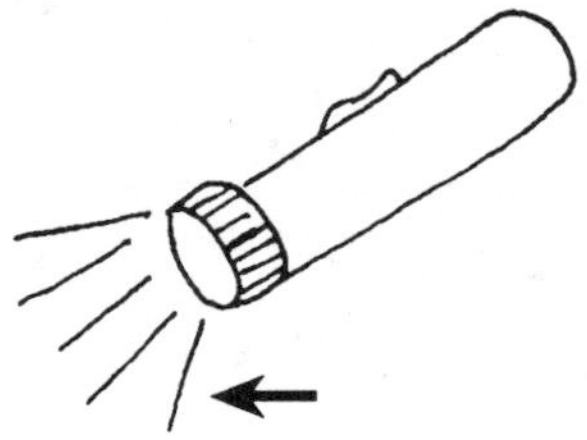

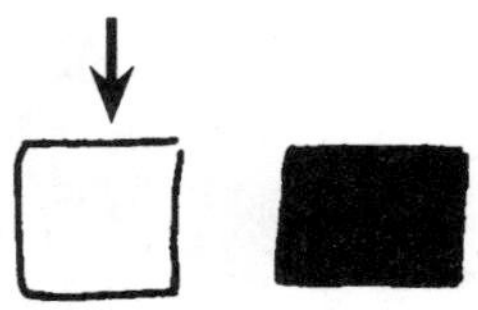

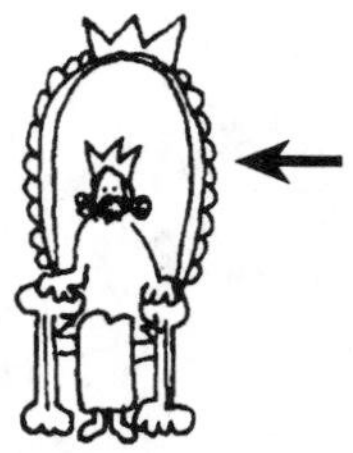

*ee* says /ē/ as in *tr<u>ee</u>*.

⬭ it.

| | |
|---|---|
| feel<br>keel<br>feet | deep<br>deer<br>been |
| jeer<br>peep<br>jeep | sleep<br>sheep<br>sheet |
| three<br>thrill<br>tree | peel<br>prick<br>peek |
| steep<br>sweep<br>sweet | cheese<br>cheer<br>chess |

Read, write, and ⬭ it.

| | | | |
|---|---|---|---|
| tree<br>_ _ _ _ | | | |
| teeth<br>_ _ _ _ _ | | | |
| wheel<br>_ _ _ _ _ | | | |
| queen<br>_ _ _ _ _ | | | |
| cheese<br>_ _ _ _ _ _ | | | |
| feed<br>_ _ _ _ | | | |
| feet<br>_ _ _ _ | | | |

*ea* says /ē/ as in *ea*r.

⬭ it.

| | |
|---|---|
| lead<br>leak<br>leaf | drum<br>clean<br>dream |
| reap<br>read<br>real | bead<br>beak<br>deed |
| seal<br>seat<br>seed | stem<br>seam<br>steam |
| track<br>three<br>treat | seat<br>seem<br>eats |

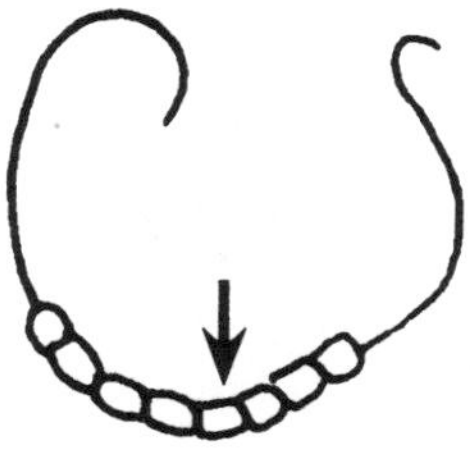

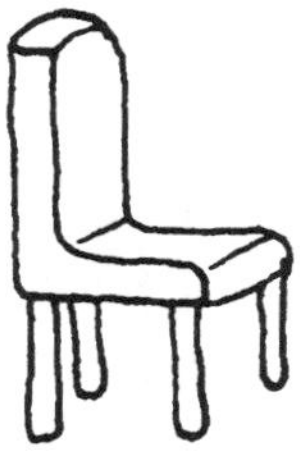

Read, write, and (circle) it.

| | | | |
|---|---|---|---|
| ear<br>_ _ _ |  |  |  |
| beak<br>_ _ _ _ |  |  | 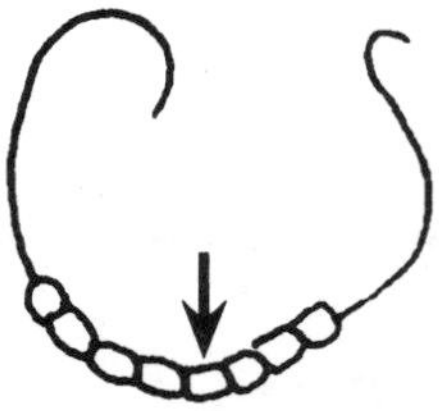 |
| treat<br>_ _ _ _ _ |  |  |  |
| clean<br>_ _ _ _ _ |  |  |  |
| speak<br>_ _ _ _ _ |  |  |  |
| meal<br>_ _ _ _ |  |  |  |
| steam<br>_ _ _ _ _ |  |  | 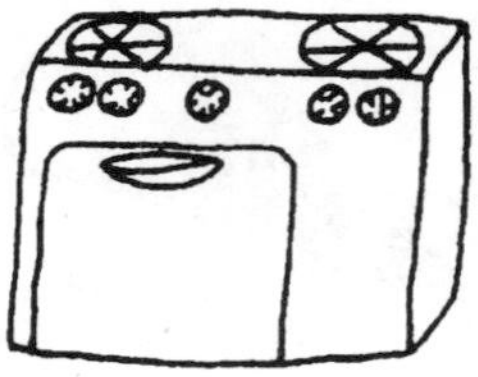 |

Match and write it.

| tree | speak | queen | steam | sweep |
| --- | --- | --- | --- | --- |
| read | deer | sheep | ear | dream |

| | Spell. | | | Write. |
|---|---|---|---|---|
| | br tr | ee at | | |
| | b t | ee e | ch th | |
| | s sw | a ea | l t | |
| | ch cl | ea oa | n m | |
| | f j | ai ee | d t | |
| | l t | e ea | f k | |
| | wh m | a ee | k l | |

Yes or no?

| | Yes | No |
|---|---|---|
| Can a jeep fly? | ☐ | ☐ |
| Will a sheep sweep the path? | ☐ | ☐ |
| Will she like a treat? | ☐ | ☐ |
| Will a chick brush its beak? | ☐ | ☐ |
| Can a twig speak? | ☐ | ☐ |
| Can I dream of fun? | ☐ | ☐ |
| Will a queen sit on a leaf? | ☐ | ☐ |

X it.

| | |
|---|---|
| The tree has a leaf. ☐<br>The tree has a meal. ☐ |  |
| Sal has a ship in the jeep. ☐<br>Sal has a sheep in the jeep. ☐ |  |
| Jim can beat a drum in the street. ☐<br>Jim can beat a drum in the tree. ☐ |  |
| The queen has a treat on the seat. ☐<br>The queen has teeth on the seat. ☐ |  |
| Tim can sweep up the dump. ☐<br>Tim can sneak up on the deer. ☐ |  |
| The king eats with the whale. ☐<br>The whale reads with the dog. ☐ |  |
| Dave dreams of a big meal. ☐<br>Dave cleans up a big mess. ☐ |  |

# Lesson 11

*ai* and *ay* say /ā/ in *p<u>ai</u>l* and *p<u>ay</u>*.

*ai* is at the beginning or in the middle of a word.
*ay* is at the end of a word.

◯ it.

| | | | |
|---|---|---|---|
| | seal<br>sail<br>sat | | sail<br>snail<br>snore |
| | peel<br>beam<br>pail | | hay<br>here<br>heat |
| | team<br>track<br>train | | step<br>stain<br>stay |
| | meal<br>nail<br>name | | play<br>clay<br>peek |

it.

rain o train?
stair or share?
pay or pail?
play or day?
stain or stay?
play or pay?
sat or sail?
trail or tail?
hay or hail?
stay or stair?

Read, write, and ◯ it.

| | | | |
|---|---|---|---|
| stay<br>_ _ _ _ | 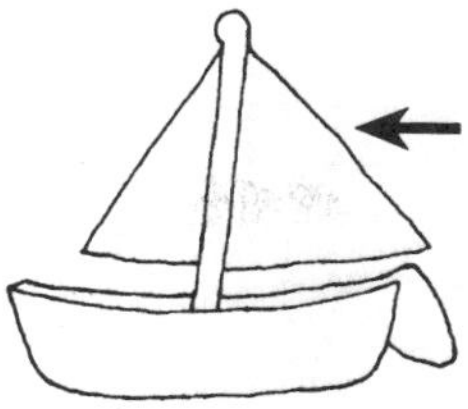 |  | 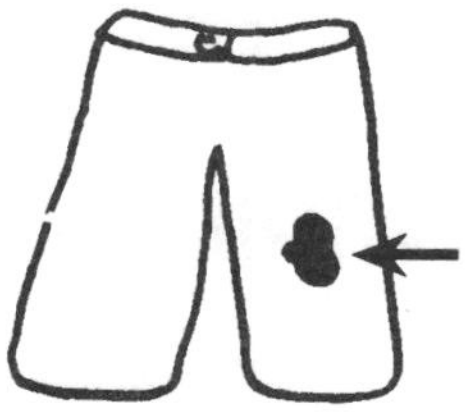 |
| pail<br>_ _ _ _ |  | 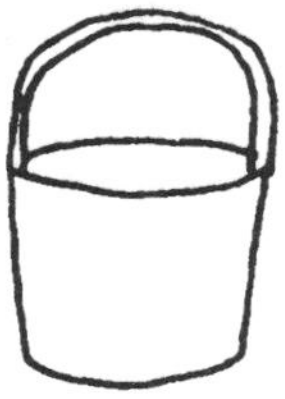 | 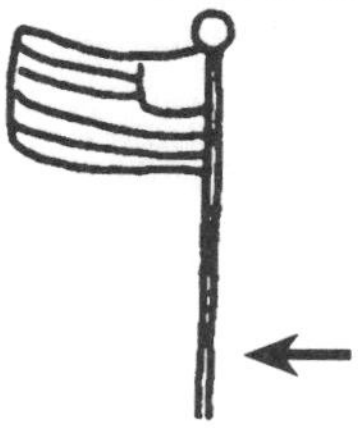 |
| hair<br>_ _ _ _ |  |  |  |
| tail<br>_ _ _ _ |  | 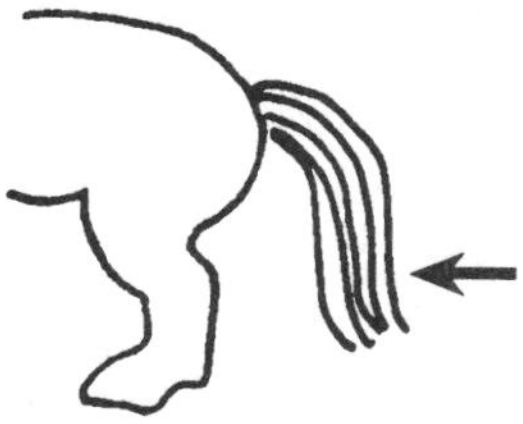 |  |
| chain<br>_ _ _ _ _ | 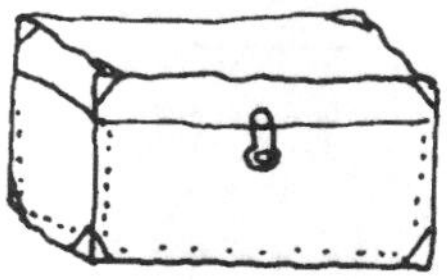 |  |  |
| stair<br>_ _ _ _ _ | 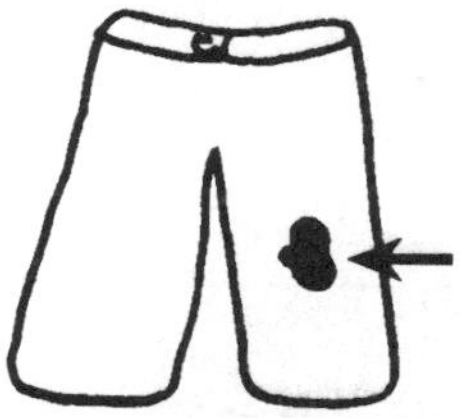 |  |  |
| hay<br>_ _ _ |  |  |  |

Match and write it.

| | | | | |
|---|---|---|---|---|
| chain | nail | stay | stain | rain |
| play | day | hay | clay | pail |

| | Spell. | | | Write. |
|---|---|---|---|---|
| | p b | ea ai | l t | |
| | ch th | ee ai | r t | |
| | s n | ea ai | t l | |
| | ch th | ai ee | m n | |
| | h n | ai ay | m r | |
| | r gr | ee ai | u n | |
| | tw tr | ay ai | n m | |

Yes or no?

| | Yes | No |
|---|---|---|
| Is hay made of hair? | ☐ | ☐ |
| Will a nail play with me? | ☐ | ☐ |
| Can you drive a jeep in the rain? | ☐ | ☐ |
| Will a chain eat on the street? | ☐ | ☐ |
| Do sheep swim on a train? | ☐ | ☐ |
| Can we try to clean a stain? | ☐ | ☐ |
| Is it a treat to stay in the rain? | ☐ | ☐ |

X it.

| | | |
|---|---|---|
| Rain hits the mail. | ☐ |  |
| Rain hits the meal. | ☐ | |
| The train stays on the track. | ☐ |  |
| The train stops on the treat. | ☐ | |
| Glen has his feet on the train. | ☐ | 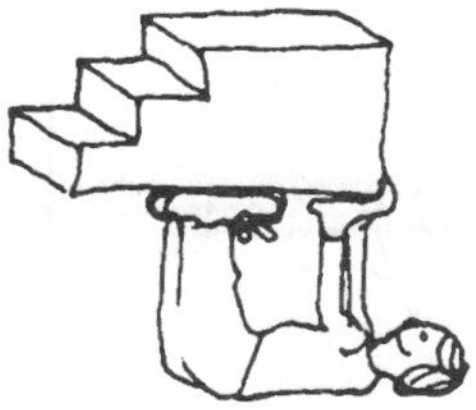 |
| Glen has the stairs on his feet. | ☐ | |
| The sheep hangs its tail in the rain. | ☐ |  |
| The sheep has hay on a plate. | ☐ | |
| Jean will sell hay at the shack. | ☐ |  |
| Jean will sail in a pail. | ☐ | |
| The dog plays on its chain. | ☐ |  |
| The dog will stay on the chair. | ☐ | |
| Steve stays in the rain for a day. | ☐ |  |
| Steve plays on the jeep this way. | ☐ | |

Write it.

*oa* and *ow* say /ō/ as in *boat*  and *blow*. 

*oa* is at the beginning or in the middle of a word.
*ow* is at the end of a word.

 it.

| | |
|---|---|
| row<br>glow<br>rope | grow<br>goat<br>gait |
| bow<br>boat<br>blow | read<br>raid<br>road |
| three<br>throw<br>tow | flat<br>fleet<br>float |
| show<br>slow<br>snow | coat<br>crow<br>coal |

◯ it.

road or roast?
blow or boat?
toad or tow?
row or crow?
coat or coast?
got or goat?
soap or snow?
bow or blow?
throat or throw?
beat or boat?

Read, write, and (circle) it.

| | | | |
|---|---|---|---|
| snow<br>_ _ _ _ |  |  | 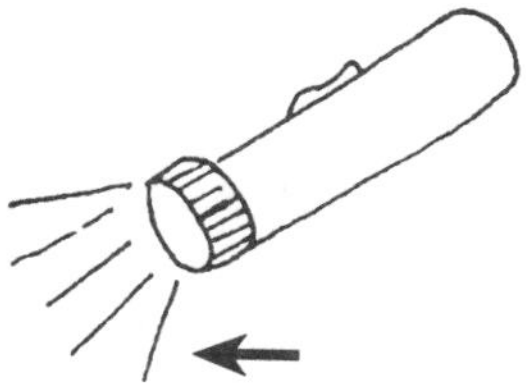 |
| roast<br>_ _ _ _ _ |  |  | 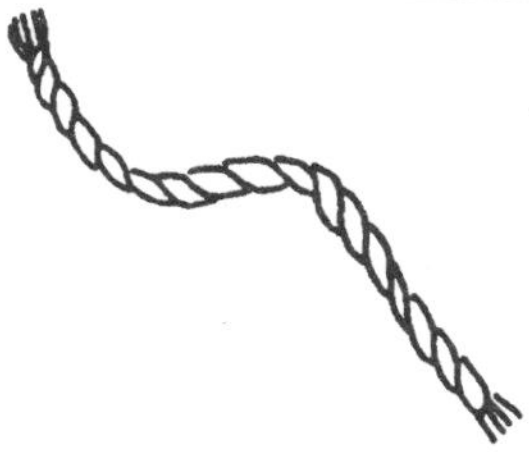 |
| blow<br>_ _ _ _ |  |  |  |
| float<br>_ _ _ _ _ |  |  |  |
| mow<br>_ _ _ | 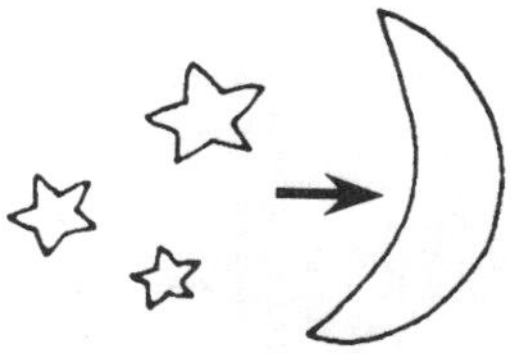 |  |  |
| boat<br>_ _ _ _ |  |  |  |
| toast<br>_ _ _ _ _ |  |  |  |

Match and write it.

| snow | goat | boat | throw | mow |
| --- | --- | --- | --- | --- |
| coat | blow | soap | slow | toad |

| | Spell. | | | Write. |
|---|---|---|---|---|
|  | bl dr | oa ow | | |
|  | s r | ai oa | p d | |
|  | t c | oa ea | ze st | |
|  | sn sw | ay ow | | |
|  | th thr | ee ow | | |
|  | r t | oa ea | p d | |
|  | c g | ow oa | t st | |

Yes or no?

| | Yes | No |
|---|---|---|
| Can you mow a roast? | ☐ | ☐ |
| Can a toad blow its nose? | ☐ | ☐ |
| Will a coat grow? | ☐ | ☐ |
| Can I row a boat in the rain? | ☐ | ☐ |
| Will a goat go to the show? | ☐ | ☐ |
| Will soap float on a dry road? | ☐ | ☐ |
| Can snow be thick and deep? | ☐ | ☐ |

X it.

| | | |
|---|---|---|
| Pat will row the boat. | ☐ |  |
| Pat will throw the boat. | ☐ | |
| The toad will fry the meat fast. | ☐ |  |
| The log with the toad floats. | ☐ | |
| Pam likes to roast a hot dog. | ☐ |  |
| Pam hates beans on toast. | ☐ | |
| We will clean the sails of the boat. | ☐ |  |
| We gave Ned a clean coat. | ☐ | |
| The goat eats soap. | ☐ |  |
| The goat is slow to read. | ☐ | |
| The chick will mow the grass. | ☐ | 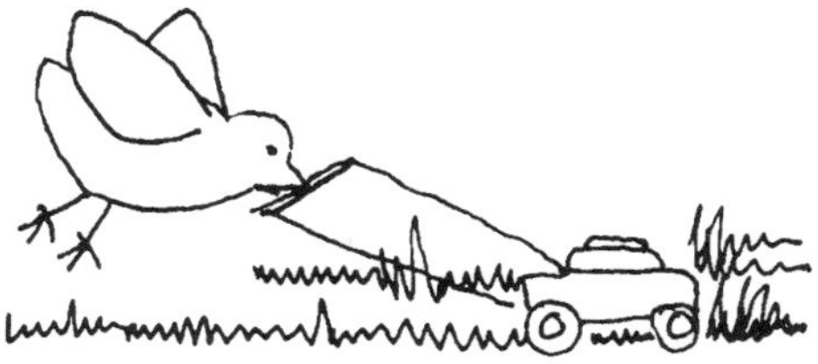 |
| The chick will mop up the glass. | ☐ | |
| The snow blows in the road. | ☐ |  |
| The snow blows on the roast. | ☐ | |

Write it.

*ee* and *ea* say /ē/.
*ai* and *ay* say /ā/.
*oa* and *ow* say /ō/.

 it.

| | |
|---|---|
| sail<br>seal<br>seat | cheat<br>chase<br>cheese |
| sled<br>sleet<br>sleep | street<br>spree<br>spray |
| roast<br>reach<br>beach | read<br>braid<br>bride |
| float<br>fleet<br>flock | three<br>throw<br>treat |

◯ it.

wheel or whale?

cheap or clean?

teeth or teach?

row or ray?

roast or reach?

speak or spray?

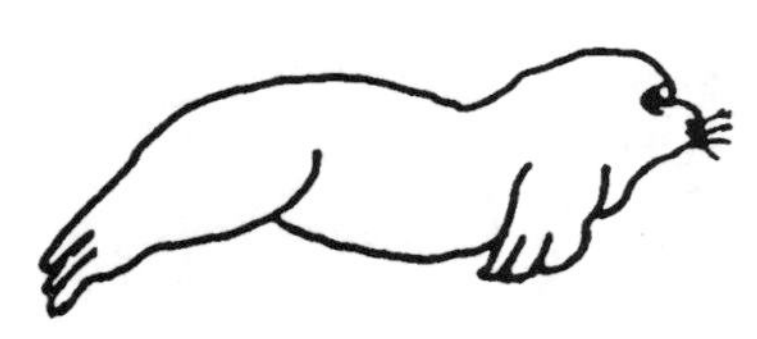

seal or sail?

paint or pain?

sneak or snail?

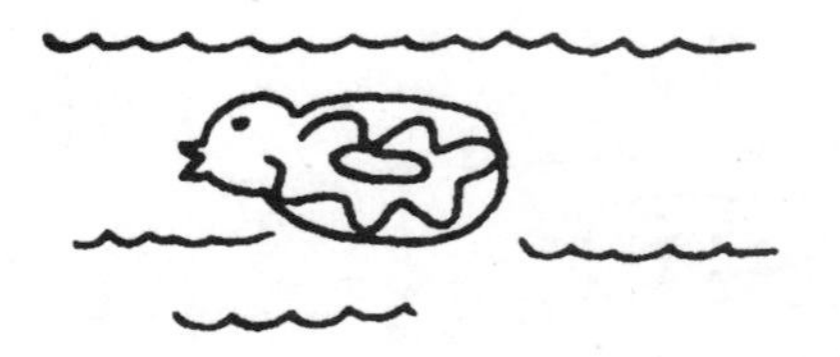

feet or float?

Read, write, and (circle) it.

| | | | |
|---|---|---|---|
| braid<br>_ _ _ _ _ |  | 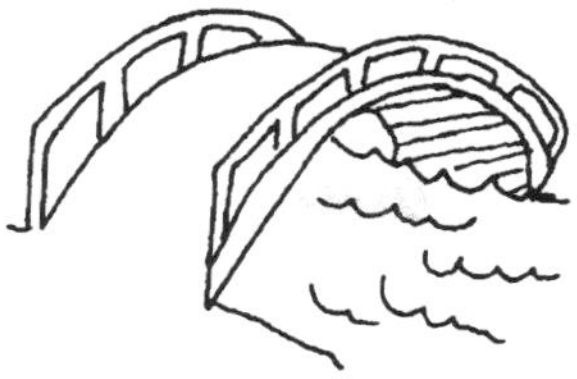 |  |
| sleep<br>_ _ _ _ _ |  |  |  |
| seal<br>_ _ _ _ |  |  | 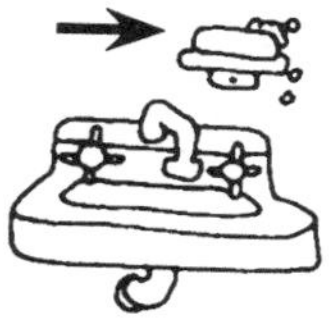 |
| eat<br>_ _ _ |  |  |  |
| spray<br>_ _ _ _ _ |  |  |  |
| chair<br>_ _ _ _ _ |  |  |  |
| float<br>_ _ _ _ _ | 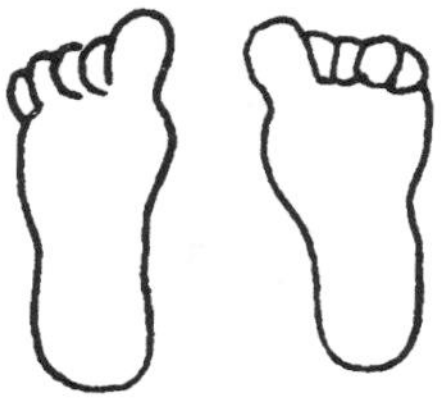 |  |  |

Match and write it.

| wheel | mean | spray | seal | cheese |
|---|---|---|---|---|
| row | paint | chair | braid | reach |

| | Spell. | | | Write. |
|---|---|---|---|---|
| | sh s | ea ai | l t | |
| | ch wh | oa ee | t se | |
| | p pl | ai ay | nt t | |
| | f fl | oa ee | n t | |
| | spr sp | ow ay | | |
| | sl sh | ee ai | b p | |
| | t r | ea oa | ch t | |

Yes or no?

| | Yes | No |
|---|---|---|
| Can you braid a nail? | ☐ | ☐ |
| Will I use my teeth to eat meat? | ☐ | ☐ |
| Will a train have a wheel? | ☐ | ☐ |
| Can you teach a toad to paint? | ☐ | ☐ |
| Will a seal sweep the road? | ☐ | ☐ |
| Can you roast snow? | ☐ | ☐ |
| Can Fred spray with a hose? | ☐ | ☐ |

X it.

| | |
|---|---|
| The goat will fly to the lake. ☐<br>The coat will fly to the land. ☐ | 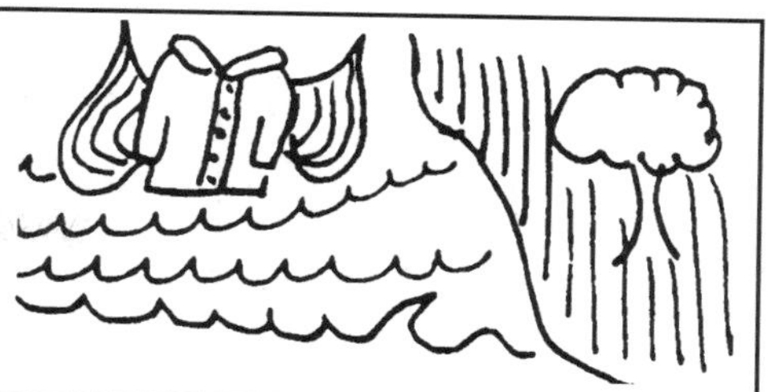 |
| The goat has its teeth in the roast. ☐<br>The goat has its feet in the road. ☐ |  |
| The flakes of snow float by. ☐<br>The slow boat rows by. ☐ |  |
| Pat can reach the chain. ☐<br>Pat can read in the chair. ☐ |  |
| Jean sneaks into show and tell. ☐<br>Jean shows me the snake. ☐ |  |
| Joan dips the brush in the pond. ☐<br>The mean brush dips Joan in the paint. ☐ |  |
| The toad swings in the rain. ☐<br>The toad sings on the train. ☐ |  |

Write it.

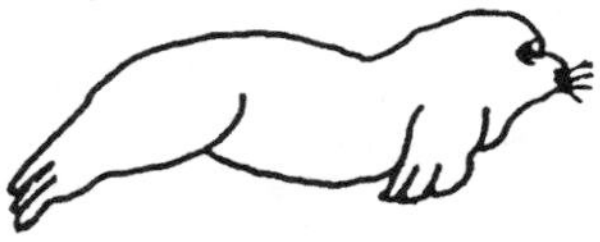

**Book 3 — Posttest**

(Teacher dictated. See Key for Books 1 to 5.)

| | |
|---|---|
| 1. spray<br>spree<br>stay<br>play | 2. share<br>sheer<br>shack<br>shore |
| 3. reach<br>rain<br>raise<br>roast | 4. wheat<br>wheel<br>whale<br>waist |
| 5. chain<br>cheat<br>chair<br>coach | 6. soak<br>sneak<br>snore<br>snail |
| 7. moan<br>mean<br>meet<br>main | 8. flee<br>float<br>flay<br>flow |
| 9. paint<br>pain<br>poach<br>peach | 10. toast<br>teach<br>taste<br>teeth |

*For further practice, see Book 3½, pp. 113–120.

**Book 3 — Posttest**

(Teacher dictated. See Key for Books 1 to 5.)

1.

2.

3.

4.

5.

6.

Read, and then write the word.

1. I put on a mask and say,
   "Trick or tr______________."

2. I like to coast on my sled
   in the deep sn______________.

3. When I use the stove, I like to
   bake a c______________.

4. When you eat a meal, you sit
   on a ch______________.

5. Please do not pull the dog
   by its t______________.

6. When I go to sleep, I have
   a dr______________.

Read and ⬭ the word.

# What Am I?

1. I can grow quite big. I give lots of shade. If you have a rope, you can make a swing in me. I have green leaves. I am a

   train.
   tree.
   tray.

2. I am white. You may not like to brush me, but you must. I help you bite your meat. Take good care of me. I am your

   teach.
   team.
   teeth.

3. At times you will row me. You may put up a sail and glide on the lake. I float well. If you do not swim, do not tip me. I am a

   bow.
   boat.
   boast.